# Little Bird Dog and the Big Ship

## *The Heroes of the Vietnam War: Book One*

Written by
Marjorie Haun

Illustrated by
Stephen Adams

*AuthorHouse™*
*1663 Liberty Drive*
*Bloomington, IN 47403*
*www.authorhouse.com*
*Phone: 1-800-839-8640*

*Published by AuthorHouse 4/11/2012*

*ISBN: 978-1-4685-6059-6 (sc)*

*Library of Congress Control Number: 2012904374*

*Any people depicted in stock imagery provided by Thinkstock are models,*
*and such images are being used for illustrative purposes only.*
*Certain stock imagery © Thinkstock.*

*This book is printed on acid-free paper.*

*Because of the dynamic nature of the Internet, any web addresses or links contained in this book may have changed*
*since publication and may no longer be valid. The views expressed in this work are solely those of the author and do not*
*necessarily reflect the views of the publisher, and the publisher hereby disclaims any responsibility for them.*

authorHOUSE®

# DEDICATION

Little Bird Dog and the Big Ship is dedicated to the American Servicemen and women who served during Operation Frequent Wind, with a special salute to the personnel of the USS Midway. This book is also dedicated to Bung Ly and his family, as well as the countless warriors and citizens of Vietnam who allied themselves with America and fought with us for the cause of freedom during the hard years of the Vietnam War.

# FORWARD

Young heroes abound throughout America. Some chose to serve our nation in uniform. They often do so anonymously, content in the knowledge that they are making a difference, are making ours a safer nation in which to live and raise our families.

Some of those young heroes served on the USS Midway, America's longest-serving aircraft carrier of the 20th century. Nearly 200,000 young men (their average age was 19) answered their nation's call aboard Midway, often in times of crisis or conflict.

Their devotion to duty in Operation Frequent Wind stands apart as the Navy's largest humanitarian deployment in our nation's history. They set personal safety aside to rescue more than 3,000 South Vietnamese refugees in two days in 1975. In each refugee they made a future defined by freedom and prosperity in America possible. It became another example of "Midway Magic," their unprecedented legacy that stands today as a symbol of the ideals and values that makes our nation great. They make us proud.

**Scott McGaugh**
**Marketing Director**
**USS Midway Museum**

Tikka-tikka, zing!

Men with machine guns spotted the little Bird Dog airplane on the runway of beautiful, but chaotic and noisy, Con Son Island. Bullets were whizzing out of palm tree thickets lining the runway, and past the little airplane. Tikka-tikka-tikka! South Vietnamese Air Force Major Bung Ly was escaping with his wife and five young children. "Mother," asked Diep, the oldest daughter, "what is happening?"

"We are taking a ride in Daddy's airplane."

"Why? Where are we going?" pleaded the girl.

"Shhhh," said Mrs. Ly. "Just get in, fast!"

Mrs. Ly pushed the children into the plane while her husband started its engine. His eyes were wide with concentration. He had to save his family. The children were whimpering in fear. Tikka-tikka-tikka, zing! The sound of machine gun bullets ripping past the little Bird Dog stung the ears of the terrified Ly children.

The gigantic aircraft carrier, USS Midway, was cruising on the waters of the South China Sea. It had become a big rescue ship for Operation Frequent Wind. When the American Forces left Southeast Asia, the enemies poured into South Vietnam, taking over its towns and cities, and making threats to the people who had helped the Americans. The deck of the Midway was no longer a landing strip for jet fighters, but was now a haven for refugees from the mainland. The frightened evacuees boarded big transport helicopters, and skilled American and Vietnamese pilots flew them to safety on the deck of the Midway. Hundreds of innocent South Vietnamese people were saved by the pilots flying the big helicopters called Super Stallions.

The flight deck of the Midway was crowded with helicopters, equipment, and hundreds of refugees who were being guided to safety by the crewmen of the gigantic ship.

South Vietnam had been a peaceful nation and its people were very kind to America. But enemies from the North fought for years trying to overrun the beautiful, tropical country which was home to farmers, fishermen, and merchants. The American Military went to South Vietnam to help their government fight invaders from the North who wanted to take over everything and force the people to live in a way they did not want to live. After many years of war, the Americans were ordered by their government to leave. Sadly the enemies from North Vietnam took over the country. Thousands of good and peaceful people from South Vietnam were rescued, and the Aircraft Carrier Midway became their temporary home.

The Cessna O-1 Bird Dog airplane was not made to carry seven people. It was almost too heavy to take off from the little island. But Major Bung Ly was an expert pilot. He managed to get the little Bird Dog into the air. And by zigging and zagging this way and that in the little airplane, Bung Ly evaded the bullets of the enemy machine guns. The Ly children were crying as the airplane zoomed up from the runway at Con Son Island. The green tracers and the constant "tikka-tikka" from the machine guns, had frightened and bewildered the five Ly children. Mrs. Ly calmed them. "Do you know what that sound reminds me of?" she whispered in a sweet and encouraging voice, "The fireworks of Tet." Her soothing words drew their memories back to the New Year's celebrations they loved so much.

"Remember the bright colors in the sky, and the popping of the fire crackers?" The cries of the children became quiet. "Remember the blooming flowers; the peach trees and the mandarins in full blossom? Remember when we were happy?" Mrs. Ly's gentle voice soothed her children, and helped relieve the panic in her husband's heart as he gripped the controls of the little Bird Dog, and guided it over the uncertain waters of the South China Sea.

"Wake up, now!" Just hours earlier Major Bung Ly's voice boomed into the ears of his children, "Get dressed! We must go!" The children rubbed the sleep from their eyes. Their father had never before sounded so strict, or so frightened. "We cannot take anything. Just come, come with me!" The family left their home, their possessions, and the life they had known, and followed Major Ly to where he kept the little Bird Dog. They did not know that once they had boarded the airplane, things would be changed forever. And their lives would be as open and danger-filled as the great ocean which now shimmered below.

"Daddy, what is that?" asked the oldest boy, Binh, as he leaned forward to look out of the front window of the airplane. "Is that a ship?"

"Yes," replied Major Ly, "a very big ship."

"Will they shoot at us?" the boy asked quietly. Major Ly paused before he answered.

"No! No, they won't shoot at us."

"Is it an American ship?" asked Mrs. Ly.

The children in the back of the little Bird Dog sat up high to look at the ship that was growing bigger as the airplane neared.

The flight deck of the Aircraft Carrier Midway was crowded with helicopters, crewmen, and many desperate people. Pilots in helicopters escaping from South Vietnam asked for permission to land on the runway, but it was so cluttered that in order to make room for more helicopters, other empty helicopters had to be pushed overboard and into the ocean.

Captain Larry Chambers wanted to save as many people as possible. His big ship had room for the helicopters because they needed only a small area on the deck to make a vertical landing. No jets or airplanes were allowed to land on the Midway because they needed a long runway. The Midway's landing strip had become a parking lot for helicopters ferrying the rescued people from South Vietnam.

It was late in the day and the crew was getting the refugees settled into their rooms on the lower decks. The Vietnam War was over, and the USS Midway was getting ready to return to America.

Captain Chambers stood on the bridge of the Midway. One of the officers was looking at the sky with a pair of binoculars. "What on earth?" gasped the officer.

Captain Chambers responded, "What are you talking about?" The officer handed the binoculars to Captain Chambers. "Unbelievable!" he exclaimed. "Try to contact the pilot." Captain Chambers looked hard through the binoculars. "If he's a friend, we'll need him to ditch the airplane, and the raft will have to pick him up."

As the little Bird Dog got closer to the big ship, Major Bung Ly recognized that it was an American aircraft carrier. He knew all about aircraft carriers, but he had never landed on one. He looked down at the Midway and he could see the crowded runway, and the many people huddled on its decks.

"Will we be able to land on that ship?" asked the middle son, Dai.

"It is too crowded," said Major Ly.

Major Ly took a stubby pencil and a ragged piece of paper from a box and handed it to his wife.

"We cannot land with all of those helicopters on the deck. They must know our situation."

The crew of the Midway looked up at the little Bird Dog as it passed right over the runway. One crewman thought he saw something falling to the deck and he ran to pick it up. The note written by Mrs. Ly was caught by a gust of wind and blown right over the side of the ship.

Captain Chambers came down from the bridge and was standing on the flight deck. "Have you made radio contact with that plane?" he asked.

"No." answered a crewman. "But the pilot tried to drop something when he passed over the last time."

"When you establish radio contact, you tell him that he's going to have to ditch the plane. There is no more room on this ship."

Major Bung Ly and his wife felt worried when they looked down at the Midway and the crew was doing nothing except looking up at them. "Write another note," Bung Ly told his wife tensely. "They don't know we have children aboard." Mrs. Ly wrote another note and again, Major Ly circled the plane and passed low over the deck of the Midway. Mrs. Ly folded the note very tightly and dropped it out of her window.

"No! I lost it. It blew over the side again!" Mrs. Ly was near tears and the oldest Ly children were quietly sobbing, doing their best to be brave.

"What can we do, Daddy?" asked Binh, the oldest boy.

"One more time," replied Major Bung Ly. "We will try one more time to drop a note. If they do not get the note we will have to go back to South Vietnam. It is too dangerous to land this plane with all of those helicopters on the runway."

"What will happen if we go back home, Daddy?" asked Diep, the oldest daughter.

Bung Ly said nothing, and focused his eyes toward the big ship.

"What's he doing?" Captain Chambers questioned the crewman with the binoculars as the little Bird Dog circled again flying just a few feet over the men and helicopters on the deck. They watched as a small white object dropped from the sky. Mrs. Ly's note found its way to the deck, but was fluttering in a breeze that threatened to take it out to sea, just like the others.

The crewman ran hard and stomped his foot on the object before it could be blown away.

"Is he prepared to ditch that airplane?" Captain Chambers said impatiently. "There's no room for him to land on the deck."

The crewman walked to Captain Chambers and unfolded the note.

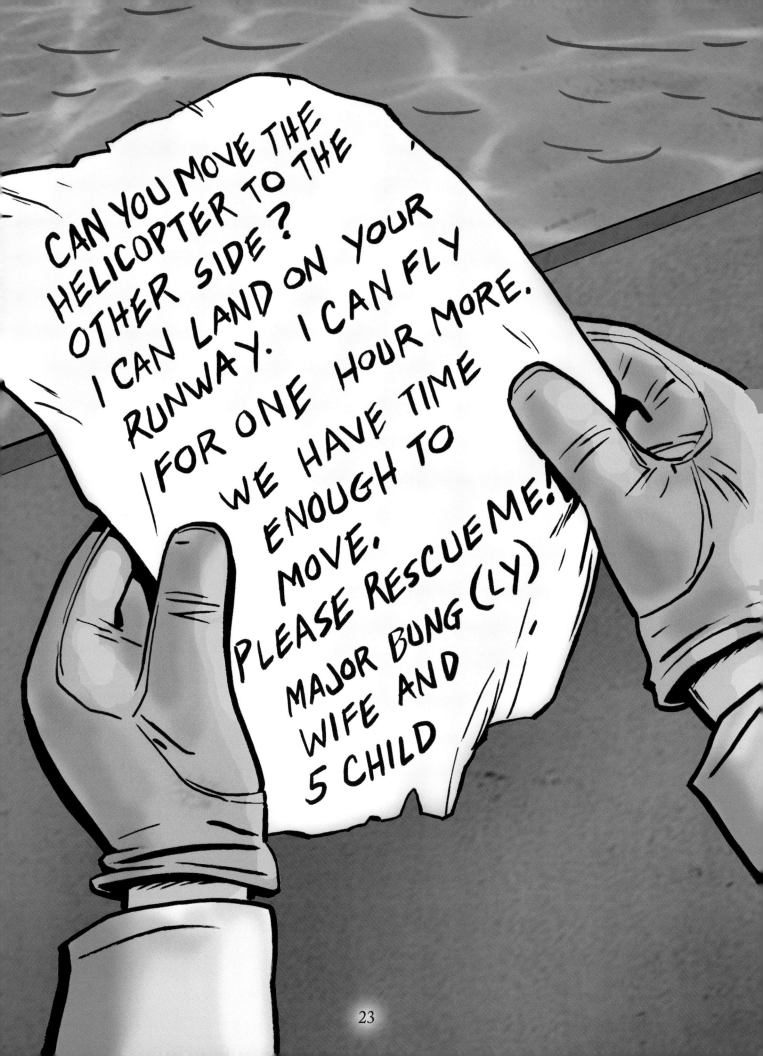

"He can't ditch." said the crewman weakly.

"Why not?" demanded Captain Chambers.

The crewman looked directly into Captain Chamber's eyes and said, "There are children on board."

Captain Chambers took the note from the crewman. He looked at it for a moment and then stepped out onto the runway of the Midway. "Clear the decks!" he roared!

The men on the flight deck and sailors from other parts of the ship gathered quickly to carry out the Captain's orders. They pushed helicopters to the sides of the runway. There was still not enough room on the runway for the little Bird Dog to land. Captain Chambers ordered the men to push the helicopters over the side of the ship and into the sea.

The Huey helicopters were important to the Americans. They supplied the troops with the things they needed. The Hueys once had moved strong men into combat zones, and evacuated wounded men to military hospitals. These hardworking helicopters were pushed into the ocean and lost forever. The Hueys were special to the men of the Midway. But the little Bird Dog was carrying something much more special, much more precious, than big expensive machines.

Major Bung Ly was flying the little Bird Dog in wide circles around the Midway. The Lys were all looking anxiously down at the big ship.

"Why are those men pushing things into the ocean?" asked Mai, the youngest daughter.

"I think they're making room for us," said Bung Ly in an excited voice. "They must have gotten the note."

"Will you be able to land this airplane, dear?" Mrs. Ly asked her husband, "You've never landed on a ship before."

"I hope so," was his whispered answer.


Rain had begun to fall and the runway was shiny and slick. The men of the Midway saw the little Bird Dog circle one last time. They could see it far off the end of the ship as it straightened its path, and leveled its wings. Everyone was very quiet; they looked worried as their eyes tracked the airplane in its slow descent from the sky towards the end of the runway.

The men of the Midway watched breathlessly as the little plane approached. The only sounds were the hum of the little Bird Dog's engine, and the crackle of rain spattering on the runway.

"Close your eyes! I will tell you when to open them." Mrs. Ly ordered her children. Major Ly held the controls of the little airplane so tightly that his hands quivered. His eyes stared hard at the runway. He chose a point in the middle of the runway exactly where he wanted to land the little Bird Dog. He brought the nose of the airplane up, slowed its engine, and in a deed of expert piloting, touched down perfectly. The too-heavy airplane landed on the precise point at which he had aimed seconds earlier.

"You can open your eyes!" Mrs. Ly cried in a happy voice!

Men on the flight deck ran out to meet the plane before it had completely stopped. They grabbed the wings and tail section to make sure it did not go off the other end of the runway and into the water.

The crew, who had been silent only moments earlier, broke out in cheers and shouts of welcome as the little Bird Dog gently delivered its grateful payload to the safety of the big ship.

Men in uniforms and safety gear surrounded the airplane. One of the men opened the door and helped Mrs. Ly and the children out of the cockpit. Captain Chambers opened the pilot's door and welcomed Major Bung Ly to the USS Midway and congratulated him on his perfect landing.

The children were picked up by crewmen who checked to make sure they were all right. Major Bung Ly and his family had become heroes to the heroic men of the Midway.

April 30ᵗʰ, 1975 had been a very long day for the men of the USS Midway. As the sun began to drop over the South China Sea, hundreds of South Vietnamese refugees settled into their temporary home on the ship. Captain Chambers and his crew were so touched by the bravery of Major Bung Ly and his wife and children, that they created a fund that, by the end of the day, had enough money for the Ly family to make a new life in America.

# EPILOGUE

Operation Frequent Wind is remembered as a heroic effort by the American forces in Vietnam, to evacuate American personnel, prisoners of war, as well as our friends, the South Vietnamese people, out of the country before it was taken over by the Communist regime of North Vietnam. Thousands of innocent lives were spared because of the efforts of the United States Military, and the men of the Midway. Sadly, many of our South Vietnamese friends did not escape to the safety of America. But thousands of people were able to make new lives in America and enjoy freedom and opportunity they had never before thought possible. The Ly family eventually settled in Florida and has enjoyed their life in America for nearly 40 years. The happy endings made possible because of the efforts of the American Military and Operation Frequent Wind are but some of the many great stories of the Heroes of the Vietnam War.

\* \* \* \* \* \*